LUCAS

2021

Life

Every Day

Mission Possible

Waverley Abbey Resources is a trading name of CWR.
© CWR 2020
Published 2021 by CWR, Waverley Abbey House, Waverley Lane, Farnham,
Surrey GU9 8EP, UK
Tel: 01252 784700 Email: mail@waverleyabbeyresources.org
Registered Charity No. 294387 Registered Limited Company No. 1990308
Unless otherwise indicated, all Scripture references are from The Holy Bible,
New International Version (Anglicised edition), copyright © 1979, 1984,
2011 by Biblica (formerly International Bible Society).
Concept development, editing, design and production by CWR.
Front cover image: blackdiamond67
Printed in the UK by Linney.

MIX
Paper from
responsible sources
FSC® C015900
www.fsc.org

WAVERLEY ABBEY
RESOURCES

Trading name of **CWR**

How to get the best out of *Life Every Day*

HERE ARE A FEW SUGGESTIONS:

- Ideally, carve out a regular time and place each day, with as few distractions as possible. Ask God what He has to say to you.

- Read the Bible passages suggested in the 'Read' references. (As tempting as it is, try not to skip the Bible reading and get straight into the notes.)

- The 'Focus' reference then gives you one or two verses to look at in more detail. Consider what the reading is saying to you and what challenges that may bring.

- Each day's comments are part of an overall theme. Try to recall what you read the previous day so that you maintain a sense of continuity.

- Spend time thinking about how to apply what God has said to you. Ask Him to help you do this.

- Pray the prayer at the end as if it were your own. Perhaps add your own prayer in response to what you have read and been thinking about.

Join in the conversation on Facebook
facebook.com/jefflucasuk

He is alive!

Read:
**Matthew 28:16–17
1 Corinthians
15:1–28**

FOCUS

*'Then the eleven
disciples went to
Galilee, to the
mountain where
Jesus had told them
to go.' (Matt. 28:16)*

B efore we head for Antioch, there are some other
locations that we need to visit. Our first is a hillside
in Galilee. At first glance, the scene seems absurd.
Eleven people gather in a rural setting. None of them
are powerful or influential, and the absence of Judas
reminds us they have already experienced betrayal and
suicide in their midst. They had scattered when their
leader was arrested. Now, their attempts at worship are
a mixture of faith and doubt. They are told that they are
to change the world with their message. The very idea
seems delusional and utterly impossible. But look at
the twelfth figure in the meeting: it is Jesus, risen now
from the dead.

Pause for a moment. The truth of the resurrection
can lose its impact, because we are so familiar with
the story. The disciples were meeting a man who had
been in the grave for three days. There had been other
examples of resurrection in Scripture, in the ministries
of Elijah and Elisha, and there are three instances of
the dead being raised in Jesus' ministry – the widow's
son, Jairus' daughter, and Lazarus (Luke 7:11–15,
8:49–56; John 11:38–44). But the raising of Jesus was
unique in history because, unlike those individuals
whom I have just mentioned, He would never taste
death again. It was His presence, and His promise to
be always with the Eleven that made all the difference.
Today, this moment, Jesus is alive. We are weak – but
He is strong. His resurrection changes everything.

**Prayer: This very second, You are alive, the risen,
ascended, glorified Christ – and You are with me and for
me. I worship You. Amen.**

He is the King

Read:
Matthew 28:16–18
Daniel 7:13–14

FOCUS

'Then Jesus came to them and said, "All authority in heaven and on earth has been given to me."'
(Matt. 28:18)

Ask a Christian what the heartbeat of the gospel message is, and you'll probably get a variety of answers, ranging from 'God is love' or 'Everyone needs rescuing from judgment' to 'Jesus wants to get you into heaven' or perhaps 'You can live a more satisfying life if you know Jesus.' There are elements of truth in all of these statements. But contained in the Great Commission is the very essence of the message that Jesus instructed the disciples to declare: Jesus is King, now. Bow the knee, now, to His good, living reign, and obey. With these instructions, Jesus was identifying Himself as the 'ancient of days' – the One who was 'given authority, glory and sovereign power; all nations and peoples of every language worshipped him' (Dan. 7:14).

Paul picks up this theme as he writes to the Philippians; Jesus is exalted above all, and so, 'at the name of Jesus every knee should bow, in heaven and on earth and under the earth' (Phil. 2:10). This was the message that would ultimately be shared with the Gentiles in Antioch, years later: it was the 'good news about the *Lord* Jesus' (Acts 11:20: my italics).

I share this because, as we will see, it is possible that the Eleven did not do what they were told, at least in a timely manner. And I am reminded today that I am called to walk with a Jesus who is not an advisor or coach, but the King, who is also my friend. And I am also called to invite others to place themselves under His good, loving, perfect reign and rule.

I am called to walk with Jesus

Prayer: I humbly, gladly bow the knee, King Jesus. You reign. Reign in me. Amen.

To all the nations

Read:
Matthew 28:19–20
Matthew 10:5–6

FOCUS

'Make disciples of all nations, baptising them in the name of the Father ... the Son and ... the Holy Spirit ... teaching them to obey everything I have commanded you.' (Matt. 19–20)

In his depiction of the ministry of Jesus, Matthew paints a picture of a Messiah who comes almost exclusively to the Jewish people, the 'lost sheep of the house of Israel'. In his accounts, Jesus prohibits His disciples from engaging in mission to non-Jews, the Gentiles. Matthew's Jesus had contact with Gentiles, but they are incidental. But all that changes after the resurrection in Matthew's Gospel – now, the commission includes all people, everywhere. The initiative for global mission comes, not from the Church as a good idea, but from Jesus Himself. I make this point because, as we will see, the Early Church was slow to respond to that command to engage in worldwide mission. There is much that we don't know about the first years of the Church, and we can only speculate as to why the great worldwide mission effort didn't begin earlier. But for now, let's agree that we need to pray for and support those who spend their lives engaging in missional projects far from home. They pay a heavy price as they leave their families for an uncertain life in a culture quite different from their own. Regular readers of *Life Every Day* will know that I have called for prayer for our missionary heroes before, and I do so again today. As they sacrifice in their response to the Great Commission of Jesus, they are often forgotten. They are often out of sight, sometimes serving in hostile situations, and so they can easily be out of our minds, and our prayerful back-up.

Prayer: I pray for those who serve around the world. Grant them strength, protection, joy, and success as they serve You. Amen.

A people of His presence

Read:
Matthew 28:18–20
Isaiah 43:1–13

FOCUS

'And surely I am with you always, to the very end of the age.'
(Matt. 28:20)

There is a pattern of request and response that I have noticed throughout the years of my journey with Jesus. Often, when I pray about a question that bothers me, or seek guidance about a specific decision or direction, the answer that comes back is simply this: 'I am with you.'

The Gospel of Matthew begins with the coming of 'Immanuel... God with us' (Matt. 1:23), and ends with the promise of Jesus that He will be with His people, always. And how they needed that assurance. In the years that followed, they would face incredible persecution because of their loyalty to Christ. Jesus affirmed cosmic authority and omnipresent presence, a claim and promise that only God could make. He has all authority, calls us to go to all nations, teaching disciples to obey all His commands, and promises He will be with us for all time.

He didn't promise an easy journey; on the contrary, disciples of Jesus are told they will face hatred and threats. He didn't say they would escape the trials of life because, He said, in this world we will have trouble. But this is His pledge, to all who seek to follow Him: we will never, ever, be alone again, at any point in eternity.

Christianity is not just about following specific principles or holding particular beliefs; it is about living our lives arm in arm with Jesus, and navigating our days by faith, affirming that He will never abandon us. May that truth, and the reality of that promised presence, strengthen our hearts today.

Prayer: I am not alone. Today, may I know the strength and empowerment that comes from Your being with me, eternal Lord Jesus. Amen.

Learning but not learning

FOCUS

'Then they gathered around him and asked him, "Lord, are you at this time going to restore the kingdom to Israel?"' (Acts 1:6)

I t must have been the most incredible experience, to spend six weeks under the tutelage of a teacher who had recently been raised from the dead! And that is exactly what the disciples experienced. I wonder what they discussed? All we know is that the main theme was the reign of God – the kingdom, the main theme of Jesus' teaching ministry prior to the cross, which was still key now, after the resurrection. Look again. Six weeks. And then comes a stunning question about the kingdom and Israel. After all that they had heard, they are still locked into the thought that their mission was all about Jesus rescuing Israel from their Roman oppressors (restoring what was old). They thought it was about their nation rather than the entire world, and the full expression of the kingdom would be in that current time, with them on the thrones in Jerusalem (Mark 10:37). Of their question, John Calvin said 'There are as many errors in the question as words.'*

Regular readers of *Life Every Day* will know that I have referred to this nationalistic, 'military Messiah' thinking a lot, and I do so again here, because it helps us understand some of the conflicts the Early Church experienced, and their hesitation about reaching the Gentile population of the world.

We will explore this more, but for now, let's ask ourselves: are we ignoring any commands that Jesus has clearly given to us? Or are there truths which we once held onto, but we are no longer applying to our lives?

Prayer: Lord, help me to listen, ponder, apply and remember what I learn from You in life. Amen.

the main theme was the reign of God

*Stott, J. R. W., 'The message of Acts: the Spirit, the Church & the World' (Leicester, England; Downers Grove, IL: InterVarsity Press, 1994), p. 41

Read:
Acts 1:7–8
Romans 12:1–2

Expectations shaped by culture

We saw yesterday that, in the culture of Jesus' day, there was a very strong expectation a Messiah would come to rescue Israel, and that from that point, Jews from around the earth would gather in the Holy City in what was thought of as a 'pilgrimage of nations'. And so when Jesus said, 'Go', rather than 'Invite them to come', there would have been confusion amongst the disciples. A mission to Jerusalem would be expected, even though Jesus had been crucified there, so it would be dangerous. Jesus was also sending them to Judea, where they had been rejected; to the hated Samaritans, who the Jews considered to be 'half-breeds'; and to the wider world, including Rome: a mission to Gentiles. Kent Hughes says, 'The words were not only spiritually revolutionary, but socially and ethnically unheard of.* Culture was still shaping their thinking.

How does culture shape *our* thinking? Let's heed the call to have our thinking shaped by the work of the Spirit.

To ponder: Can you think of other examples from recent history where culture was wrong, or where it might be wrong now?

*Hughes, R. K., *Acts: the Church afire* (Wheaton, IL: Crossway Books, 1996), p.17

Bouncing Forward

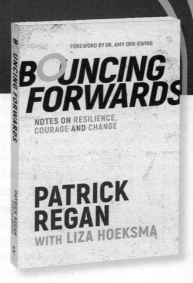

Suffering, trauma, anxiety, grief – so many of us experience these. Given all that has gone on over the past year, it's likely that we've all experienced a struggle or major set-back to some degree recently. So where do we go from there?

In this new, relatable book from Patrick Regan, discover what it looks like to face these things as a Christian.

Bouncing Forward will help you understand what true resilience really is, and how it goes beyond bouncing back. By looking at stories, words of wisdom and personal insights from Patrick, you'll be able to understand how the times when you may feel you're going backwards can actually springboard you forward. Nothing you go through is ever wasted.

'I want to bounce forward, demonstrating emotional agility when my feelings are threatening to overwhelm me.'

– Patrick Regan

Patrick Regan is CEO of Kintsugi Hope, which he founded with his wife, Diane. His recent books include Honesty Over Silence (Waverley Abbey Resources), which seeks to open up conversations around topics that some find difficult.

Partnership, power and journey

Read:
Acts 2:1–4
Matthew 4:18–22

FOCUS

'They saw what seemed to be tongues of fire that separated and came to rest on each of them.' (Acts 2:3)

I am grateful for my Pentecostal heritage, but I am afraid that, over the years, some have placed far too much emphasis on the gift of speaking in tongues. I do acknowledge this is a wonderful gift, one that enables me to talk to God when I can't think of a single intelligible word to say, which is often. But we should always remember the power of God came at Pentecost to give these trembling, hesitant disciples the courage and energy needed for their mission. And that power was given to a commissioned people called to travel, to go. The power arrived during the harvest feast of Shavout. When the Holy Spirit fell, tongues of fire came, a reminder of when the pillar of fire led the people out in the Exodus and journey to the promised land. The fire was also in the cloud that had rested on the tabernacle each night, a sign of God's presence with a tent people, on the move with Him. So this is what we are – a people travelling with God, empowered by God, knowing God's dwelling presence. When Jesus called His disciples, He used the words, 'Follow me', an invitation to journey and change.

Later in these notes we will explore this more, but for now, let's consider the challenge – are we settled, static in our faith, or are we still moving, growing, available to the God who is going places in His purposes and wants us to go with Him? Are we still changing and learning, faithful pilgrims, especially when our Christian walk is an uphill struggle?

an invitation to journey and change

Prayer: If I need it, Jesus, unsettle me, that I might never become static, attached to where I am, satisfied with progress so far. Amen.

Babel reversed

It is a strange scene, as people in the crowds hear the gospel in their own languages. The curse of the Tower of Babel was reversed on the Day of Pentecost. At the beginning, God pronounced all of creation good. But the first eleven chapters of Genesis describe the unfolding increase of sin in the world. It begins with Adam and Eve failing in the garden of Eden in chapter 3, and this is closely followed by the first murder in chapter 4, when one of their sons kills the other. God's creation begins to deteriorate as humanity then attempts to exert sovereignty over God and tries to become like God.

So the Tower of Babel event is the climax of humanity's attempts at self-sovereignty. The human family was then scattered, and people completely divided. The Tower of Babel represents a turning point in humanity's terrible downhill slide, and confusion of languages was the result. Now, at Pentecost, that curse was broken. The gospel would go out, as a sign of what was to come, first to the Jews and then to every tribe and nation. The Church, a new, just, united community, was birthed.

We reflect what happened that day in our missional activities, and in the way we approach the scourge and evil of racism. We are called to be a community that models racial reconciliation, where prejudice is unthinkable, because now we are all one in Christ Jesus. The world is crying out to see a living example of racial harmony and we, the people of God, need to step up.

Prayer: Prince of Peace, may I reflect Your heart to create a people of all nations, together in peace, united in You. Amen.

Read:
Acts 2:5–13
Genesis 11:1–9

FOCUS
'When they heard this sound, a crowd came together in bewilderment, because each one heard their own language being spoken.' (Acts 2:6)

The components of Church

Read:
Acts 2:42–45
Ephesians 4:11–16

FOCUS

'They devoted themselves to the apostles' teaching and to fellowship, to the breaking of bread and to prayer.'
(Acts 2:42)

Living in beautiful Colorado, where the snow-topped Rocky Mountains stand proudly on the landscape, I occasionally hear a particular comment when talking with people about the importance of church. 'Don't need it', sniffed one gentleman recently, with a look of disdain on his face. 'The mountains are my church. When I am out there, I feel close to God, and I don't need any church service to help me get closer.' There is a British version of this as well: people who feel that an occasional gathering in a coffee shop or pub is church. But when we look at the infant Church in Jerusalem, while their structure was quite different from ours – no buildings of their own, for a start – we would be wrong to think their 'church' was totally informal and haphazard. Despite the sudden, massive influx of converts, they quickly got organised, and their sense of shared community was intense. Certain activities were prioritised, such as teaching, prayer, breaking bread, and fellowship together. They quickly developed a leadership structure, and exercised church discipline, because those who identified themselves as followers of Jesus were expected to behave in a certain way. They shared resources and saw miracles performed.

Church can be exciting or dull, inspiring or draining. It is not a consumer product, designed to be exactly what we would prefer. But while the way we express church can be incredibly diverse, the truth is that we are called to be the people of God together.

Prayer: I am grateful to be part of a new creation people, Lord, Your people. When life in Your family is a challenge, grant me tenacity and grace. Amen.

Structured and informal

Read:
Acts 2:42–47
Malachi 3:1–4

FOCUS

'Every day they continued to meet together in the temple courts. They broke bread in their homes...' (Acts 2:46)

The early Christians initially spent a lot of time in and around the Temple of Jerusalem. Luke ends his Gospel with the ascension of Jesus, and then describes the disciples being 'continually at the temple, praising God' (Luke 24:53). And then in the early part of Acts, we see the disciples gathering in the Temple courts, (Acts 2:46) going there at the time of prayer (Acts 3:1), and meeting in Solomon's Colonnade (Acts 5:12). Perhaps this was why a number of priests came to faith in Christ (Acts 6:7). It is thought that the disciples did this because the Temple courts were the ideal place for preaching, and because they saw the Temple as belonging to Jesus. He had thrown the moneychangers out, and now they saw Him as the Temple's rightful owner. Knowing the promise of Malachi, perhaps they looked forward to the time when Jesus would come and take full control of Israel and the Temple too.

But they also met together in their homes. The late John Stott saw this as a healthy picture of discipleship. He didn't think the disciples would have participated in the sacrifices, but he does see them taking part in the structured prayers of Temple life – complementing this with house to house fellowship. In Stott's words, 'There is no need to polarise between the structured and the unstructured, the traditional and the spontaneous. The Church needs both.'* Gathering for celebration and worship, nurtured by small group engagement – that's a great combination.

Prayer: Thank you for the opportunities that I have to gather with Your people, Father. Amen.

*Stott, J. R. W., *The message of Acts: The Spirit, the Church & the World*, (Leicester, England; Downers Grove, IL: InterVarsity Press, 1994), p.85.

Growing... but ?

FOCUS

'We will turn this responsibility over to them and will give our attention to prayer and the ministry of the word.'
(Acts 6:3–4)

Three years have passed since the Day of Pentecost. The Church is still largely in Jerusalem and is exclusively Jewish, and the apostles have moved their operation to Jerusalem. The church there is experiencing growth and tension – the two usually go together. But there have been no attempts to take the gospel further, to Judea, Samaria, and the ends of the earth. An ancient legend says the apostles were instructed to stay Jerusalem-bound for twelve years, and then to go out and spread the gospel, but even if that is true, it didn't happen that way. Peter was involved in actively spreading the gospel but, with rare exceptions (Acts 10) he only preaches to Jews, as Paul later confirmed (Gal. 2:7). John goes with Peter to Samaria in a preaching trip, reported in Acts 8, but it is others, apart from the Twelve, who would properly spearhead the global outreach. Perhaps this was because the Twelve felt that they should maintain leadership from Jerusalem.

Whatever the reason, the Great Commission was not being fulfilled, and we know for certain that when Gentiles were reached, the Jerusalem leaders struggled with the theological and social issues that Gentile conversion raised. Here is a question, not a statement: again, is it just possible that success in Jerusalem had caused some complacency? Whether that is true or not, I am asking, in my walk with Jesus, am I still daily available to His great purposes, diligent in discipline, and running the race to win?

Prayer: Save me from complacency, Lord. Here I am, wholly available, today. Amen.

Unwavering

An extract from the introduction of Jen Baker's latest book

One of the most profound truths in the Bible is that regardless of how we came into this world – whether by love, passion or violence – we were chosen. God is intentional and at the moment of creation you were not only His first choice, but His best choice. At birth, He knew the number of hairs on your head (or lack thereof) and the number of days before you. God is responsible for bringing us into the world, but what we do with that time – and the legacy we choose to leave – is solely our responsibility.

Choice was created at the birth of Creation. The first Hebrew word of the Bible means 'in the beginning' and the second means God (*Elohim*), with the third word, *bara*, meaning 'created'. Any type of creation, whether we are creating a meal or a memory, involves choice. Therefore, Elohim chose, before time was established, to express His love by appointing mankind as the recipient of His love; because love without an object to love is unfulfilled, empty and void of purpose. In other words, you are God's desire!...

My prayer is that as you read, fear will lose its grip, faith will come alive, and purpose will be realigned… positioning you for a lifetime of relentless, kingdom pursuit.

This is your time, and this is your choice – make it an unwavering one.

Want to keep reading?
Visit **waverleyabbeyresources.org.uk/products/unwavering** to continue.

Gathering clouds: Stephen

Another year has passed. The Church has navigated some challenges: arrests, beatings, and internal conflict. Then Stephen is arrested, condemned, and stoned to death in a hideous lynching. As I read about Stephen's terrible death, I am humbled. Perhaps, like me, you have wondered how you would fare if faced with the choice of execution or denying Christ? The question may be futile because we don't have the grace now to face it. Should it come, we trust God would strengthen us.

It has been famously said that the blood of the martyrs is the seed of the Church, and as we will see, that is proven by all that will follow. For now, let's pause and quieten our hearts, as we remember that around the world today people are still paying the ultimate price for following Jesus. There is often little or no media coverage when Christians are killed. But if overlooked by the press, they must not be forgotten by their worldwide Christian family. Today, let's remember them in prayer.

To ponder: How might we pray specifically for our brothers and sisters in the persecuted church?

Scattering and first steps

Read:
Acts 8:1–4
Job 19:25

It must have a terrifying time for those early Christians, as 'great persecution' broke out against the Jerusalem church. The church was shattered as everyone, except for the apostles (who probably stayed in what they saw as the headquarters to maintain leadership) headed for wider Judea, Syria, Phoenicia and beyond. When they resettled, as Messianic Jews they became part of local synagogues. But they were still not safe in their scattering, because a zealot called Saul, given authority by the High Priest, determined to hunt them down and bring them back for trial and punishment.

FOCUS

'Those who had been scattered preached the word wherever they went.' (Acts 8:4)

But now look again at this situation, from another angle. God was obviously not the architect of the persecution, but He redeemed the situation. The upheaval and scattering of those refugee believers provided the catalyst for the wider spreading of the good news about Jesus, which would directly lead to the birth of the church in Antioch, where mission to Gentiles ignited. And it was during his journey to Damascus, in his enraged search for Christ-followers there, that Saul encountered Jesus. Ultimately, of course, Saul would become Paul, the great apostle to the Gentiles. God seems to have an amazing ability to turn what is meant for evil into good. David sleeps with Bethsheba, a terrible sin, but Jesus comes from their lineage. And the cross is the ultimate example. Intended to silence Jesus in death, it becomes the way of life for all. God is the redeemer.

Prayer: You are alive, and You are my redeemer. Take my struggles, even my mistakes, and redeem them, Lord, for Your purposes. Amen.

He
redeemed
the situation

Step 2: Philip and God's patience

Read:
Acts 8:4–8
Acts 8:14–17

FOCUS

'Philip went down to a city in Samaria and proclaimed the Messiah there.'
(Acts 8:5)

Yesterday we saw that God redeems situations that He did not design. He used the persecution of the Church to scatter the believers, which then led to the gospel being shared. One of those scattered was Philip, one of the seven who had been chosen to oversee food distribution back in Jerusalem. The persecution had catapulted him from administration into mission. The call to preach in Samaria was not fulfilled by one of the Twelve, but by the chap originally asked to oversee the food bank, a wonderful picture of God's ingenuity and ability to get the job done! It was a bold step, because of the age-old enmity between Jews and Samaritans; the parable of the Good Samaritan is the best example of storytelling about those hostilities. It was only a small step, however. The Samaritans who heard Philip's message would already have observed the Mosaic law, and so none of the complications that emerged later, when Gentiles came to faith, would surface.

When news of Philip's campaign reached Jerusalem, Peter and John were sent to investigate. It is a theme that we will revisit, but here we see an incredible work of God, an outreach to Samaria that was not on the Jerusalem church's missional radar. They must play catch-up with what God was doing, by launching that investigation. Slowly, gradually, the Church is inching towards the idea that Gentiles could be part of the Christian family, but other events would have to unfold first. God is patient. I am grateful.

Prayer: For Your loving kindness and long-suffering nature towards me, Lord, I give thanks. Amen.

Step 3: Peter and John in Samaria

Read:
Acts 8:14–25
Acts 9:32–43

Peter had experienced a lot of patience from Jesus. Prone to talking without thinking, he received a stinging rebuke when he suggested the cross was not a good idea. And his sword-swinging in the garden Gethsemane ended with an unintentional ear amputation, a blunder that Jesus quickly fixed. Sent initially on a fact-finding mission from Jerusalem, we see him inching forward in his thinking. The ambassadorial mission turned into a time of prayer ministry. And then he and John returned home but preached in 'many' Samaritan villages on the way. Once again, let's remember the cultural situation, summed up in six words in John's Gospel: 'For Jews do not associate with Samaritans' (John 4:9).

Peter then goes to Joppa, a mainly Jewish area, but we find him staying with Simon, who was most likely a follower of Jesus. Simon would have been seen as a 'bad' Jew, because he was a tanner, one of the so-called 'sinner' trades in Jewish thinking. His work as a tanner, dealing with dead animals, would have made him ceremonially unclean. Over a period of years, Peter has taken baby steps – first to Samaritan Jews, then to compromised Jews like Simon. Gradually, Peter's heart and mind are being opened up. A cataclysmic revelation is about to come, but not before God slowly, carefully, prepares Peter for it. Wisdom is found in the journey with Jesus, if we are open to it. What are we learning as we walk with Him? As we learn, apply and remember, He can take us further.

FOCUS

'After they had further ... testified about Jesus, Peter and John returned to Jerusalem, preaching the gospel in many Samaritan villages.'
(Acts 8:25)

Prayer: What do you want me to know right now, Father? Teach me Your ways. Amen.

Wisdom... in the journey

Step 4: God the choreographer

Read:
Acts 10:1–8
John 10:22–30

FOCUS

'He is staying with Simon the tanner, whose house is by the sea.' (Acts 10:6)

Perhaps another four or five years have passed. Remember, a decade has come and gone, and although there has been some progress, no Gentile has yet been converted (the Ethiopian eunuch baptised by Philip was probably a Jew heading to Jerusalem for worship). As we will see, Peter was still labouring under the burden of thinking that he could not associate with Gentiles. And so, like a chess player, the Holy Spirit organises some interlocking experiences to bring solid confirmation that the Gentiles were welcome in the Church. Cornelius was a 'God fearer', which means that, while he was a Gentile, he worshipped the God of the Jews. This was just another teetering step forward, because Cornelius already had Jewish links. Tomorrow, we'll look at the vision Peter was given, but that vision would be confirmed by the visit of Cornelius's delegation – he had been supernaturally informed of Peter's name, the city where he was staying, the name of the man he was staying with, and the location of the house. And the timing of the visit was yet further confirmation, because they came as Peter was pondering the vision, and the Holy Spirit told him how many callers were at the door. All of this is the equivalent of God raising His voice, making His will known, very loudly and clearly. When wanting direction, I wish that God would always make what He wants known so obvious, but it is not always like that. But when God does raise His voice, let's hear it and respond.

Prayer: I want to be sensitive to Your voice, and available to Your direction. Help me, faithful God. Amen.

Step 5: The vision

Read:
Acts 10:9–23
Acts 11:4–17

FOCUS

'"Surely not, Lord!" Peter replied. "I have never eaten anything impure or unclean."' (Acts 10:14)

As a LifePlan coach, I walk clients through a two-day intensive review of their life history, take inventory of where they are at now and plan accordingly. And I take careful note of turning points: events they entered as one person, and emerged from as someone else, the event was so significant. Peter's rooftop vision was one of those episodes. It changed him forever, and changed the course of Church and global history. Peter refers to this vision elsewhere (Acts 11:4–9), as it had such an impact. Kent Hughes describes what happened and why: 'When God told Peter, "Do not call anything impure that God has made clean," God was confronting Peter's prejudice. Peter had bound all the peoples of the world, except for his own race, into one loathsome bundle.'*

I write this a few days after the tragic killing of George Floyd, murdered by a police officer in Minnesota. We are all aware of the global reverberations from that act of brutality, with protests, removal of statues, and in-depth conversation about the pandemic of racism that still infects our culture. Racism in Peter's heart could have prevented the Church from sharing the gospel beyond Judaism, and Christians would have remained a Jewish sect. God had called Israel to be distinctive, but never superior or arrogant. Hopefully, this is a turning point for our world as we confront the evil of racism. And it could be a turning point for us as we allow God's Spirit to search our own hearts.

Prayer: If I am oblivious to racist attitudes within me, show me, Lord, that I might see people as You see them: greatly loved, made in Your image. Amen.

Visit **waverleyabbey resources.org /podcast** to listen to a podcast

*Hughes, R. K., *Acts: the Church afire* (Wheaton, IL: Crossway Books, 1996) p.149

Read:
Acts 10:23–48
Galatians 3:23–29

Step 6: God is in the house

Jesus' clear worldwide commission was to take the good news to all people, everywhere, but Peter's exclusively Jewish thinking remained – until that vision, of course. In one sentence, he summarises that exclusivist attitude: 'He said to them: "You are well aware that it is against our law for a Jew to associate with or visit a Gentile' (Acts 10:28). For centuries, this had been the prevailing rule, and as an observant Jew, he was just going along with it. Now Peter is working out the practical, social implications of the revelation that he has been given. He preaches the gospel, the Holy Spirit falls on his Gentile hearers, and it's worth noting again the reaction: 'The circumcised believers who had come with Peter were astonished that the gift of the Holy Spirit had been poured out even on Gentiles' (Acts 10:45). God was doing a new thing, and they struggled to understand it. Let's be open to the God of surprises. He is trustworthy, but not predictable.

To ponder: When did you last change your mind about a long-held view or opinion?

A potential backward step

Read:
Acts 11:1–18
James 1:22–25

FOCUS

'When they heard this, they had no further objections and praised God, saying, "So then, even to Gentiles God has granted repentance that leads to life."' (Acts 11:18).

What God does is not always welcomed with open arms by God's people. After all these steps forward, a huge backward step is taken as the believers in Judea object to Peter's actions, and tell him so when he returns to Jerusalem. Their main concern was not to the news of the conversion and baptism of the Gentile converts, but the fact that Peter had shared meals with them. Gentiles did not observe the Jewish food laws, and so table fellowship with them was unthinkable – one writer describes the idea of Jew and Gentile at the same table as 'earth-shattering'.

Peter calmly explains himself, telling his critics the whole story. And although this issue would constantly resurface, as we will see, he brought peace to the situation by choosing to respond graciously and humbly. But there is a postscript. We hear of the Jerusalem believers praising God at the news that Gentiles were now included in God's purposes and family, but that does not mean the Jerusalem church began any mission to Gentiles. As we arrive shortly at Antioch, that responsibility falls to them instead. In fact, there is no evidence that Jerusalem ever reached out to Gentiles, with terrible results. One writer describes their hesitation and says 'As a result (the Jerusalem church) lost its importance in course of time.'* Words of praise were not enough. What we really believe is what we live by, as James makes clear. Ideas might just be religious froth. Actions count.

Prayer: Save me from vague convictions that are not translated into the way I live, Father. Amen.

Actions count

*Marshall, I. H., *Acts: an introduction and commentary* Vol 5, (Downers Grove, IL: InterVarsity Press, 1980), p. 210

To the big city

Read:
Acts 11:19
Ephesians 3:14–21

FOCUS

'Now those who had been scattered by the persecution that broke out when Stephen was killed, travelled as far as Phoenicia, Cyprus and Antioch.'
(Acts 11:19)

Visiting New York, I felt a mixture of exhilaration and intimidation. The atmosphere is cosmopolitan, and it is famed for art, culture and food. The sense of intimidation came as I walked through Times Square, and the question surfaced: how on earth could these diverse people be reached for Jesus?

Perhaps that is how some Christian refugees felt when they arrived in Syrian Antioch. It was the third largest city in the Roman Empire, with a teeming population of half a million. Compare that with Jerusalem – at this time in history, the holy city had just around 30,000 inhabitants, a figure that swelled to 80,000 or so during the Jewish feasts. Antioch was beautiful, known as 'Antioch the Golden', with a main street four miles long, paved with marble. A trade centre, it boasted a busy port. Beneath the surface, it had a dark, sinister underbelly, like most cities ancient and modern. A goddess called Daphne was worshipped there – throughout the Empire, her name was associated with immorality. Five miles from the centre of the city stood a temple staffed by prostitutes who specialised in acts of depravity, all conducted under the guise of worship.

It was here, not in Jerusalem, that the doors of the Church would finally swing wide open to all – although, again, as we will see, controversy continued. God impacted this big city – and He can do the same in our villages, towns and cities. He is still the One who can do more than we can ask or imagine.

Prayer: Mighty God, with You, the greatest challenge is surmountable. Help me to remember that when the way ahead seems impossible. Amen.

Waverley Abbey College

Education that changes lives

Our programmes equip students with the skills and knowledge to release their God-given potential to operate in roles that help people.

Central to all of our teaching is the Waverley Integrative Framework. Built on 50 years of experience, the model emphasises the importance of genuineness, unconditional acceptance and empathy in relationships. The courses we offer range from certificates to Higher Education level.

Counselling

As society begins to realise the extent of its brokenness, we continue to recognise the need to train people to support those who are struggling with everyday life, providing training to equip individuals to become professional counsellors. Whatever their starting point in academic learning, we have a pathway to help all students on their academic journey.

Spiritual Formation

For those wanting to be better equipped to help others on their spiritual journey, this programme provides robust and effective Spiritual Formation training. Students engage with theology, psychology, social sciences, historical studies, counselling, leadership studies and psychotherapy.

For more information about all of our course offerings available, visit **waverleyabbeycollege.ac.uk** or **call 01252 784719**

God uses those available

Read:
Acts 11:19
Isaiah 6:1–8

FOCUS

'Now those who had been scattered by the persecution that broke out when Stephen was killed travelled as far as Phoenicia, Cyprus and Antioch.'
(Acts 11:19)

I remember the night that my call to Christian leadership was confirmed. I have talked about it before, so there is no need to repeat the story here, but the call was unmistakable. Perhaps God knew that He would have to give me a rather arresting call that would sustain me through the years to come. There have been times since when I would rather have done something else. But back then, I felt intimidated; I just could not see how someone as ill-equipped as I was could be of any use to the kingdom of God. I have since learned that God only uses ordinary, in-the-process people, mainly because nothing else is available.

We saw yesterday that the task of impacting the big city of Antioch would have been daunting. But the chosen ambassadors were not members of the Twelve, or the seven. Phillip and Peter were not the ones appointed for the task. Rather it was a group of arriving Hellenist (Greek-speaking) refugees that God used. The city was impacted as they shared the good news. The words that Luke uses in Acts tell us that Christ was proclaimed and preached in their gatherings, but He was also talked about in their everyday conversations.

Throughout Scripture there are examples of typical human reactions when God calls; fear, intimidation, incredulity, and a sense of feeling disqualified. But ordinary people in the hand of God can do great things, in His strength and for His glory. Don't exclude yourself, but make yourself available afresh.

Prayer: In my weakness, be my strength, as I offer myself for Your purposes today, gracious Father. Amen.

Experimental church

Read:
Acts 11:19–20
1 Corinthians 9:19–23

FOCUS

'Some of them, however, men from Cyprus and Cyrene, went to Antioch and began to speak to Greeks also, telling them the good news about the Lord Jesus.'
(Acts 11:20)

One of the positive results from the Covid-19 pandemic was the challenge to the Church to be flexible and innovative. Congregations that never thought of providing online worship opportunities have taken the plunge; house groups have 'met' through Zoom and Teams meetings. We have discovered that we can change. As we have seen, it took some divine acts of choreography to convince Peter that he could preach the gospel to a non-Jewish audience, but there is no mention of any angelic visions to the believers arriving from Cyprus and Cyrene. Other Christian travellers from Phoenicia and Cyprus had shown up first, and were sharing Jesus, but only with fellow Jews. Potentially, it was another backwards step. It was when the second group arrived that the revolution broke open. Perhaps those from the second group shared with Gentiles because it didn't occur to them there was anything wrong in doing so – many of them had converted to Judaism and were proselytes, so why not invite others to convert to Christ? Or their sharing might have just been the result of their overflowing love for Jesus. What they did went beyond anything that had happened before. Philip and Peter had preached to Samaritans, who practised Jewish law. Cornelius had loose connections with the synagogue and Judaism. But these anonymous evangelists shared Christ with those who had no Jewish background or links whatsoever. Let's be willing to innovate, change and experiment.

Prayer: When change comes, help me not to resist it because it is unfamiliar. Save me from being stuck in what was. Amen.

The Lord's hand

Read:
Acts 11:21–26
Isaiah 43:1–13

FOCUS

'The Lord's hand was with them, and a great number of people believed and turned to the Lord.'
(Acts 11:21)

I t is one of Luke's favourite phrases – he uses it several times in writing the book of Acts and his Gospel. Reporting the success of the anonymous refugee evangelists in Antioch, Luke says that 'the hand of the Lord was with them', an Old Testament metaphor for God's power and favour. Elsewhere, Luke says the hand of the Lord was with John the Baptist (Luke 1:66); with the apostles in providing miracles (Acts 4:30); and against Elymas the sorcerer in judgment (Acts 13:11). Now that same hand is upon these enthusiastic 'good news' believers. But let's remember these refugees had been persecuted and displaced and, as we will see, further trials were to come in Antioch. Let's affirm again God's ability to redeem our struggles. We saw that Philip's successful campaign in Samaria was the result of persecution and scattering and now the planting and growth of the church in Antioch is also the result of pain and upheaval, rather than a methodical mission plan from the church in Jerusalem. Yet in their pain, they are blessed. Perhaps you are steering your way through what has been an extended season of difficulty. Your frequent prayers for healing or relief have not been answered as you would like. But still you trust God. Thank you for doing that, and whatever else you may or may not know, let this truth somehow warm your heart today: suffering does not mean abandonment. May you know the hand of the Lord is upon you.

Prayer: Wonderful Father, today, You are with me, for me, wanting me to experience Your hand of blessing. I praise You. Amen.

Simply Church

– New Edition

By Sim Dendy

In light of all the changes that churches have faced in the last year, we're releasing a new edition of Simply Church, in which Sim has written a chapter all about being agile in response to difficult situations.

From his experience of both attending and leading churches, Sim Dendy asks some key questions about how we 'do' church, just in case there's something we could be doing differently.

Sim looks at the church as being somewhere we can encounter God, gather together with other believers, grow in our faith and knowledge of God's Word, and therefore influence the world around us – even if we can't always do all this face-to-face. While church systems are really important, nothing should eclipse the church's purpose in being God's great hope for the world.

Be encouraged as you discover just how simple church can be: how we can get connected, grow stronger, manage our resources and really make a difference.

Simply
Church.

Because it's not
meant to be this
complicated.

SIM DENDY

To find out more and to purchase,
visit **waverleyabbeyresources.org/product/simply-church**

Read:
Acts 11:22
Matthew 21:1–11

Jerusalem calling

Three hundred miles from Antioch, the church in Jerusalem heard rumours about the strange happenings in the golden city. Viewing themselves as the headquarters for Christianity, they were concerned and, from all we have learned about their attitude to the Gentiles, we can understand why. Just as Peter was sent to investigate Philip's work, now Barnabas is sent to Antioch. It is a surprising choice, because he was not one of the Twelve, but it was a wise decision. Once again, the Church is having to play catch-up with what the Holy Spirit is doing through those unnamed, unauthorised refugee evangelists. This was quite unexpected.

Years earlier, Jesus had ridden into that same holy city – the event that we celebrate this Palm Sunday weekend. The crowds waved palm branches, a symbol of Jewish (and Roman) nationalism. He came not to rescue a single nation, but to redeem a planet. That day, Jesus was what Jerusalem needed, but not what it expected.

To ponder: Can you think of times when God did something for you or through you that was quite unexpected?

Leading the investigation

Read:
Acts 11:22
Acts 4:36–37

FOCUS
'News of this reached the church in Jerusalem, and they sent Barnabas to Antioch.' (Acts 11:22)

In my view, Barnabas is one of the great heroes of Scripture, an often uncelebrated one. Back in 2013, I wrote a series of Bible notes focusing on Barnabas for *Life Every Day*, and then published a book about him (*There are No Ordinary People*, available from Waverley Abbey Resources). I will limit my comments about him here, but he played such a significant role in Antioch that we need to focus on him for a few days. Without him, we might not have the apostle Paul, the great apostle to the Gentiles who gave us a third of the New Testament. It was Barnabas who brokered a meeting between Paul (then known as Saul) with the nervous members of the Jerusalem church, anxious that Saul might have been posing as a believer to infiltrate the Church and continue his persecution. Barnabas invited Paul to co-lead the church in Antioch, from which the great missionary journeys were launched.

Barnabas was a Cypriot Levite, a landowner who led the way in generous giving when the church in Jerusalem was formed. He was also a man with a servant heart. A seasoned leader, he navigated the transition between him and Paul as gradually Paul takes the leading role in the apostolic travels. Perhaps you are an unsung hero too; you are tired in your serving, and feel a little under-appreciated. Please don't give up – and thanks for all you do. It matters – and God *always* notices. And if you know someone like this, tell them you notice what they do, and encourage them.

Prayer: Bless and strengthen those who quietly serve behind the scenes, Father, and may I encourage them. Amen.

God *always* notices

A brave encourager

Read:
Acts 9:1–31
Acts 7:54–8:3

....

FOCUS

'When he came to Jerusalem, he tried to join the disciples, but they were all afraid of him, not believing that he really was a disciple.'
(Acts 9:26)

Yesterday I mentioned that Barnabas bravely endorsed and supported Saul when he arrived to meet the church leaders in Jerusalem. Imagine how Barnabas felt when he came face to face with the primary architect of the persecution. Saul had been converted some three years earlier, but was only now contacting the apostolic group in Jerusalem. In that climate of terror, it was Barnabas who stepped up and decided to take Saul into the company of apostles. This was an action that could have been foolhardy and even disastrous. If Saul had been faking conversion so he could infiltrate the inner circle of the Early Church, he could have arrested them all on the spot, imprisoned them or worse. The infant Church would have been devastated. And as Barnabas broke ranks and introduced himself to the man who had been partly responsible for the death of the Church's first martyr, Stephen, he risked his own neck too. But Barnabas refused to be immobilised by fear.

Sometimes people who are positive, and who offer encouragement freely, can be seen as a flighty. Their cheerful, open disposition suggests to others they are not really seeing the problems that exist. But there was nothing insubstantial about encourager Barnabas. Aware of the dangers in choosing to offer a hand of welcome to Saul, he went ahead anyway. Encouragement is not just about smiles and warm words, but demands a brave heart, willing to take risks when others shrink back in fear.

Prayer: I want to be willing to take risks in the cause of love, Lord. Help me when that moment comes. Amen.

Seeing grace

Read:
Acts 11:19–30
Philippians 2:12–18

FOCUS

'When he arrived and saw the evidence of the grace of God, he was glad.' (Acts 11:23)

Some people are gifted at noticing the flaws in others. Delighted at every opportunity to object, complain or correct, they seem to spend their days muttering. And then there are others, like Barnabas, who have both spiritual discernment and an open heart, looking for the grace of God at work. He met with the new believers in Antioch – excited disciples who would not have been developed in their discipleship and would have had many rough edges in character. Nevertheless, he could see past all that to what God was doing in them.

I travel a lot, and so people often ask me the question, 'What do you think God is doing these days?' While I hopefully have a few limited insights, I would like to have a greater understanding of God's specific strategy, and then to make sure I am fully onboard with it. But 'seeing grace' is not just a leadership issue. Sometimes we can be blinded to the grace of God at work in others because of prejudice. We do not see much good in them because we focus on the negative, which we notice first, and then choose to focus on. Before long we are tempted to write them off, categorising them as bad people, oblivious to their very real character strengths.

For Barnabas, the result was celebration – he was glad. Like Paul, who writes about his friendship with the Philippians with joy and delight, Barnabas discovers grace leads us to gladness, whereas prejudice leads to pain. Have you ignored the grace of God in someone else's life?

Prayer: Father, please give me the ability to see grace, in what You are doing, and in others around me. Amen.

Avoiding legalism

Read:
Acts 11:19–30
Colossians 2:16–23

....

FOCUS

'He was glad and encouraged them all to remain true to the Lord with all their hearts.' (Acts 11:23)

It has been said there is no problem if people quite unlike us show up at our churches. The tensions arise if they *stay*, and don't become like us quickly, even though it is not God's intention that they should be like us, but like Jesus. Barnabas was moving into some tricky territory, as Gentiles were coming to faith in Christ. Now they were in the family, what steps would they need to take to stay in the family? The Early Church would constantly battle with those who insisted following Christ meant adopting circumcision and other Jewish ceremonial rituals. At this stage, nobody had discussed this, and the issue had not been settled. Barnabas could have been tempted to play it safe, and demand the Gentile converts in Antioch initially submit to those Jewish rules. But instead of leaning towards legalism, the man who was glad because he *saw* grace, made others glad as he *shared* grace. This must have been tough for him – later, as we will see, even he was to waver in his conviction about how Jewish Christians should treat Gentile believers. Barnabas was a wonderful man, but he too could make mistakes. But at this stage of his ministry, rather than placing huge importance on external ceremony, he chose to validate them because of their heartfelt love for Christ.

Legalism can attack us all. It starts when we insist that everyone does faith our way, and our personal principles are universal. Instead, we need to err on the side of grace.

Prayer: May I model grace and graciousness, Lord, and give others space to grow in what You want them to be. Amen.

Goodness and Good Friday

It is that day again, the day of the cross, and yet the day that we call 'Good' Friday. it seems odd to call a day of execution a good day. But before we consider that, notice Barnabas was described as a 'good' man, a phrase Luke used elsewhere only of Joseph of Arimathea (Luke 23:50). And Barnabas was good, not just because he did good things, but because of his openness of heart. The word means 'large hearted' – Barnabas refused to engage in narrow sectarianism. There was nothing cold in his goodness; he was not one of those puritanical, legalistic souls that one writer (rumour has it that it was Mark Twain) who described some as being 'good in the worst possible way'.

And here we pause and consider the One who gave Himself for us on Good Friday. He was and is the epitome of true goodness. But more than that, He was the pure, holy lamb of God – most linguists believe that we call this Friday 'good' because the word was originally associated with holiness. This is why the gates of the Church were thrown open to the Gentiles, because now the price had been paid by the Lord Jesus, and so they could be included in the covenant promises of God. And today, we worship and are thankful, because the radical inclusion that came through Christ's work on the cross ushered us, too, into the kingdom. And what a price it was. In Antioch, Gentiles were celebrating grace. And for us, it is a good day too, and we have a good God.

Prayer: Your outstretched arms on the cross ensured me a welcome of love, Lord Jesus. I can never repay that debt, but I worship You. Amen.

Read:
Acts 11:19–30
Matthew 27:32–44

FOCUS
'He was a good man...'
(Acts 11:24a)

Outrageous grace

He is risen! Jesus is alive! That changes everything.
Death is beaten, and new life is available. A stunning
example of the transforming power of the resurrection
of Jesus is found at Antioch. The fledgling church
there needed further leadership, and Barnabas
decided to draft Saul in as a co-pastor. But many in the
congregation in Antioch were in the city as refugees
because of the terrible persecution that had followed
Stephen's death. Saul had been one of the primary
persecutors. So the believers in Antioch may have lost
homes, livelihoods, and even loved ones because of
him. Now he was not only joining their church, but
becoming a leader. He had met the risen, ascended Jesus,
and his life had been changed beyond recognition. And
resurrection power is demonstrated in the epic grace
shown by the Antiochene Christians towards their
former nemesis – and Luke doesn't even comment on
that grace. When we truly know the risen Christ, grace
flows through our lives. Happy Easter!

To ponder: What is greatest change that God has
brought about in you?

Here come the Christians

FOCUS

'The disciples were called Christians first at Antioch.'
(Acts 11:26)

It has been said that 'Sticks and stone may break my bones, but words will never hurt me.' That is a lie. I am sure that, like me, many of you can look back at times when you were wounded by cruel words. Luke tells us the followers of Christ 'were first called Christians in Antioch'. As we'll see, Antioch was ethnically a very divided city, and the Jesus people were difficult to categorise. In a city where people kept to their own ethnic groups, here was a group whose members came from different ethnic backgrounds, and what held them together was the One they followed: so they were named after Him. If this is true, then they modelled racial harmony.

Most commentators believe being called 'Christian' was a derisive tag. The Antiochenes were famous for their sarcastic humour. A group of fanatical emperor worshippers lived there, and they were dubbed 'the *Augustianoi*'. When the Jesus people arrived, they were nicknamed the '*Christianoi*' – Christ's people. So as they navigated insult, Barnabas encouraged them to remain 'true to the Lord with all their hearts' (Acts 11:23). This was something of a life message for him – he would share similar encouragement in another city called Antioch, in Pisidia (Acts 13:43) and beyond (Acts 14:21). If you are experiencing some ridicule because you follow Jesus, you are in good company. By the grace of God, stand firm, and with those early Christians, be glad that you are worthy to suffer for His name.

Prayer: Faithful God, when others mock me because I trust You, help me to stand with clarity, confidence, and kindness. Amen.

stand firm

Read:
Acts 11:27–30
Acts 21:10–11

FOCUS

'One of them, named Agabus, stood up and through the Spirit predicted that a severe famine would spread over the entire Roman world.' (Acts 11:28)

Famine predicted and a generous response

Fly-tipping was a significant problem during the lockdown season in the early days of the coronavirus crisis, as recycling centres were closed for weeks. During a morning walk near our home, we came across an entire load of rubbish in the middle of the road, left by one incredibly selfish person. It blocked the road completely, which was shut for eight days. But the pandemic also threw up many heart-warming stories of generosity and selflessness. 'Mask trees' appeared around the country, as people provided sewn masks for passers-by. And Captain Tom won our hearts.

As a prophet warns of a devastating famine to come, the first response of the church in Antioch was not 'How will we survive', but rather 'How can we help and give?' And their thoughts immediately turned to the Christians up in Jerusalem who were likely to suffer more. This demonstrates ongoing links and respect for the church there, even though, as we have seen, they had not initiated Gentile mission. In Antioch, we see not only a charismatic church, open to the use of the gifts of Holy Spirit, but also a compassionate and concerned church, responding to the needs of the poor – a healthy balance. In the ministry of Agabus, the prophet who spoke up, we see another balance, because he prophesied into the macro situation of the coming economic challenges, as well as later speaking into the micro situation of Paul's imprisonment – and both prophetic predictions came true.

Prayer: Lord, I ask for open ears to what Your Spirit is saying, and an open heart to the needs of others rather than preoccupation with myself. Amen.

A multiracial Church

Ancient Antioch was a cosmopolitan city, an eclectic mix of cultures and ethnicities, which brought their own conflicts. When it was first constructed, it was designed as a divided city, with a wall to keep Syrians and Greeks apart. In New Testament times, at least 18 different ethnic groups were living within the city's boundaries, and a real sense of division remained, with each group mostly keeping within their own communities. I am reminded of the clear ethnically divided sections of old Jerusalem. But these early believers defied those cultural divisions. While there were tensions at times, they sought to live as a diverse group of people united around the gospel of Jesus Christ.

The leadership of the Antioch church was also ethnically mixed. Simeon Niger was one of the key people, a black leader from North Africa. His nickname is surely unfortunate because it has been used as a horrible racist term, but he served alongside Paul and Barnabas – both obviously Jewish, but also speakers of both Aramaic and Greek. There was Manaen, who grew up with privilege in the household of Herod Antipas. From North Africa (Libya) came Lucius of Cyrene, who may have been one of the initial evangelists who came to Antioch and began reaching out to Greeks. Today, when the call for racial justice is urgent, we see a portrait of what the Church should be – a multiracial family set on reaching everyone everywhere with the good news, a true light to the world.

Prayer: God of all people, everywhere, may Your people model what its mean to live together, with diversity celebrated in unity. Amen.

Read:
Acts 13:1
Matthew 5:14–16

FOCUS

'Now in the church at Antioch there were prophets and teachers: Barnabas, Simeon called Niger, Lucius of Cyrene, Manaen who had been brought up with Herod the tetrarch) and Saul.' (Acts 13:1)

How to change the world

FOCUS

'While they were worshipping the Lord and fasting, the Holy Spirit said, "Set apart for me Barnabas and Saul for the work to which I have called them."' (Acts 13:2–3)

Although, as we have seen, Gentiles were already coming to faith, this episode marks the epic beginning of the Christian Church's more intentional decision to take the gospel to the whole world, regardless of ethnicity or background.

Barnabas and Paul were taking part in the church's time of corporate fasting and worship (Jesus' teaching on private fasting doesn't condemn corporate fasting, but insists that we don't use fasting as a badge of pride). Although the directive to set the two apart for apostolic mission came from the Holy Spirit, they, together with the rest of the congregation there, received this directive while they were giving themselves to those spiritual disciplines. The inference is that the word of the Lord came through the prophets in the church. Encourager Barnabas didn't just do good things, but was filled with the Spirit, available and obedient to God. He and Saul embraced a costly and disruptive calling. The road ahead for the missionary pair was far from easy – there would a great deal of pain. Let's keep offering ourselves to the 'interruptions' of God, and express that availability through personal and corporate discipline. Frankly, I am not a great fan of fasting. I much prefer feasting. But today I am challenged to pick up that neglected discipline in my life, not to be legalistic, but to express my ongoing availability to whatever God wants from me.

Prayer: Show me what it means for me to be truly available to You, Lord, in this season of my life. Amen.

Keep up

Read:
Acts 13:1–4
Galatians 5:16–25

FOCUS

'So after they had fasted and prayed, they placed their hands on them and sent them off. The two of them, sent on their way by the Holy Spirit...' (Acts 13:3–4)

When we invited a neighbour and friend to join us for a long walk in the country, he politely declined. 'I like to walk very briskly' he said, 'And I would be worried that you wouldn't keep up.' He is probably right.

The title of the book of Acts is 'The Acts of the Apostles', but I believe it is wrongly named. Surely our study of the story of the Early Church shows the title is misleading. It would be appropriate to call this exciting book 'The Acts of the Holy Spirit', because repeatedly we see God taking steps without the involvement or knowledge of the apostles. They then not only had to play catch-up, but often had to deal with the conflict that broke out because of God's activity, which often bewildered them. As we will see tomorrow, that is not the case here in Antioch, as the church stands on the edge of a brand-new strategy. But I am challenged – am I keeping in step with the Lord, walking in the Spirit? As Paul called the Galatian Christians to walk with the Lord, he used a term that means 'to walk around with' – the verb *peripateo*, from which we get out word 'peripatetic'. This is the word used to describe those who walked around with Aristotle, learning as they travelled. Just as God walked around the Garden of Eden with the first couple, so we are called to journey daily by faith with Him. And that means keeping up. Is it possible that you and I limit God, because what He wants to do in and through us is beyond our comprehension?

Prayer: Give me discernment, Lord, to know what You are doing, and commitment too, to keep in step with You. Amen.

Read:
Acts 13:3–4
Luke 18:1–8

Partnering with God

What is the point of asking God for things in prayer? Dallas Willard taught that request sits at the heart of prayer: God wants us to ask, and be tenacious in our asking, as the parable of the persistent widow shows. Seeing as He knows all things anyway, however, why do we need to tell Him what we would like?

One answer is that God has chosen to invite us, His people, into partnership with Him in His purposes for the earth, and for our lives. That has always been the case, from the very beginning, when the Lord charged Adam and Eve with the stewardship of His creation. Here in Acts we see the church not only in prayer, but in harmony with the Lord rather than playing catch-up – we read that *they* sent Barnabas and Saul out, and then two verses later that this dynamic duo were sent by the Holy Spirit. Sent by humans, sent by God. At last – the church is in step. Today, let's not lag behind or run ahead of God, but embrace the privilege of partnership with Him – and that includes prayer.

To ponder: If a new Christian asked you for a helpful tip on prayer, what advice would you offer?

Checking the revelation

I have written before about Christians who apparently have a hotline to God. Their days are peppered by heavenly revelations and conversations with the Lord... allegedly. With unseemly haste, they dash off in a direction which then leads to disaster. Usually there is no conversation about their previous claims of divine guidance, just a rather embarrassing hush as they try to pick up the pieces. Until the next time when the Lord allegedly speaks...

I make this observation, not to be cynical or unkind, but because I have witnessed too many of these awful episodes. And God must be wearied by the countless times that His name is used to endorse foolish initiatives.

These relatively new Christians in Antioch show great maturity, as they position themselves to listen through their prayers and fasting, and in the way they check the direction they sense God is giving. We are not told how the Holy Spirit revealed the missional plan to send Barnabas and Saul out on their journey, but most scholars think it was probably through one of the prophets, like Agabus, whom we met earlier. Notice, though, they either began a new season of prayer and fasting, or continued the fast they had started, before laying hands on the new missionaries. This was a discerning, careful church. We should follow their example when we feel we have heard from God, not despising prophecies, but, to quote Paul, 'test them all; hold on to what is good' (1 Thess. 5:21).

Read:
Acts 13:1–4
1 Thessalonians 5:12–28

FOCUS

'So after they had fasted and prayed, they placed their hands on them and sent them off. The two of them, sent on their way by the Holy Spirit...' (Acts 13:3–4)

Prayer: Grant me a heart sensitive to You, Lord, ready to do Your will, carefully discerning Your voice. Amen.

Giving their best

FOCUS

*'So after they had
fasted and prayed,
they placed their
hands on them and
sent them off. The
two of them, sent on
their way by the
Holy Spirit...'*
(Acts 13:3–4)

We spent over a decade as members of Revelation Church, Chichester, and it was an exhilarating experience. A church largely made up of young people, there was such a radical sense of commitment. The worship was dynamic, and the 24–7 Prayer movement, led by one of the former fellow leaders of Revelation, Pete Greig, was birthed there, and it now has global reach. In a time of negative equity in the housing market, some people relocated at great loss to plant congregations in the region. The giving of the church was generous and sacrificial. It was a delight to be numbered among people who gave their best for the kingdom.

Under the leadership of Barnabas and Saul, the church in Antioch had flourished. An amazing year of teaching from the pair had gathered 'great numbers of people' (Acts 11:26). We have already seen their generous response to the famine fund for the church in Jerusalem. Barnabas's decision to add Saul to the teaching team had been a huge success. But now, the church in Antioch were being asked to release these anointed leaders to the wider work of taking the gospel to the Gentile world, a calling to which they willingly responded. It must have caused them great pain and concern about how the local work would fare with their two primary leaders gone for much of the time. Their response reminds me of the woman who anointed Jesus with expensive perfume, an act He celebrated as a 'beautiful thing'. When called upon, let's live and give beautifully.

Prayer: Lord, may I give according to Your will. Amen.

live and give
beautifully

Steps into the unknown

Kay and I enjoy walking, especially in the South Downs in Sussex. There are hundreds of ancient public footpaths that crisscross the hills, which provide us with endless opportunities for exploration, and a few episodes of being lost. Our times of bewilderment have ended now, though, because we bought an app that charts every footpath in the UK. I can plan our walks, find an estimate of how long they will take and what inclines we will navigate. During the walk, a helpful voice will provide step by step instructions. It is quite brilliant – our days of 'navigational tension' are over.

I would like life to be like that. While I don't want to know all the details of what is ahead, I would love greater clarity about what I should do and when. Life generally and ministry specifically involve transitions, so a chart downloaded from heaven, clearly pointing out when those junctions are and what choices should be made would be very useful indeed. No such 'app' exists.

Before we move on from this episode, notice it is only recorded that the Holy Spirit describes Barnabas and Saul being sent out to 'the work to which I have called them'. Commentators note no more specific details were included; some suggest this was like the call of Abram, who was simply told, 'Go... to the land I will show you.' Saul had known since his conversion that he was called to the Gentiles, but the details had not been inked in. Sometimes, we just take another step – and trust.

Prayer: When I am unsure about where You are leading me, Father, help me to be faithful, bold, and trusting. Amen.

Read:
Acts 13:4–5
Acts 9:1–19

FOCUS

'The two of them, sent on their way by the Holy Spirit, went down to Seleucia and sailed from there to Cyprus.' (Acts 13:4)

Visit **waverleyabbey resources.org /podcast** to listen to a podcast

Visit the Holy Land and Jordan
9-17th November 2021

Join Jeff and Kay Lucas on a life changing tour of Israel and Jordan, visiting famous sites that will transform the way you read and view the Bible, including Galilee, Jerusalem and Magdala, the home of Mary Magdalene. Capernaum and the Garden of Gethsemane are included, as well as the amazing desert landscape of Wadi Rum with its idyllic orange sands and rock formations.

Imagine sharing communion while sailing on the Sea of Galilee; exploring the ruins of Capernaum, where Jesus based his ministry; ascending Mount Nebo where Moses viewed the promised land, and sharing worship, prayer and teaching on the beach where Jesus cooked His disciples breakfast after a long night's fishing. And then there's Petra, the world famous archaeological site in Jordan's southwestern desert. Dating to around 300 B.C., it was the capital of the Nabatean Kingdom. Accessed via a narrow canyon called Al Siq, it contains tombs and temples carved into pink sandstone cliffs. Perhaps its most famous structure is 45m-high Al Khazneh, a temple with an ornate, Greek-style facade, and known as the Treasury.

Professional local guides share their wealth of historical and archeological knowledge; Jeff offers teaching as we tour, and Jeff and Kay host the entire experience - one that some travelers have enjoyed so much they have returned to do the same trip a second time!

With excellent hotels, amazing food, and the unforgettable experience of exploring the stunning old city of Jerusalem (with markets where you can haggle for a bargain) this trip will delight and inspire. Come with us!

What others had to say about the tour...

'The memories of this tour are priceless. Jeff brings to life the Bible stories in such a way that one can imagine being there in Bible times.'

'Jeff and Kay kept the momentum of the tour consistent, and the amount of places visited in a very safe and organised fashion is truly remarkable – superb!'

'Our Israel trip was both a spiritual journey and an amazing adventure. Jeff and Kay were great hosts. Our tour guides in Israel and Jordan were knowledgeable and fun.'

'The tour schedule was very manageable and allowed for people to see all the sites, wander alone or just rest. Unforgettable holiday!'

Book your place now and join Jeff and Kay from 9–17 November 2021.

The health and safety of our group members is our number one priority. Our experienced travel agents closely monitor the fast-moving coronavirus situation and are pleased that travel restrictions are being lifted or mitigated in many countries. Our tours strictly adhere to the UK Foreign Office travel advice together with the Israeli Government safety guidelines to ensure all tours operate and conform to any regulations that may be required.

For more information, visit **toursforchristians.com**

Let me tell you a story...

Read:
Acts 14:21–26
2 Timothy 3:11–12

FOCUS

'From Attalia they sailed back to Antioch, where they had been committed to the grace of God for the work they had now completed.'
(Acts 14:26)

We fast forward now about another one or two years. Saul (now known as Paul) and Barnabas have completed their first missionary journey, which we won't focus on too much here because our study centres on the church in Antioch, not Paul's wider ministry. Paul refers to this season in his letter to Timothy. In summary, it had been an amazing, challenging trip; conflict and supernatural intervention in Cyprus, response but then expulsion from another city called Antioch (there are two in Acts, Syrian and Pisidian), and a conspiracy to stone them to death in Iconium. Following another miracle in Lystra, Paul endured an attack that almost killed him. After repeat visits to some of the locations, where the two encouraged their converts to endure and stay true to the faith, it was time to sail home again to Syrian Antioch, their sending church.

The church was eager to hear their story, to find out about the fruit of the sacrifice of releasing their leaders to wider ministry. I will say more about the details of what Paul and Barnabas shared tomorrow, but for now, let's affirm the power of our stories. Testimonies used to be a regular feature in many churches. I have written about this before, but I am sad those opportunities don't happen much any more. We are strengthened and encouraged as we recount the acts of God in our lives. That is why I personally value small groups, where we share more than teaching, and explore life together.

Prayer: I pray for the church of which I am a part, Lord. May we be more than a learning centre, but a family travelling together, sharing our stories as we go. Amen.

Look what God has done

Thanking the speaker after a service where he had preached brilliantly, I felt rather rebuked for expressing my appreciation. He swiftly rejected what I had intended as genuine encouragement. 'No, no, don't thank me, it was the Lord' he insisted, pointing heavenward. Personally, if someone thanks me for something I have done, I express gratitude, and am glad of the encouragement. But it is vital that we remember that God is the source of all blessing and anointing, and the language used in this episode repeatedly affirms that. Paul and Barnabas had been 'committed to the grace of God' in Antioch. The language here echoes Barnabas's initial visit to the city, where he 'saw what the grace of God had done' (Acts 11:23). The wonderful things unfolding were the work of God, in and through them. Tom Wright comments, 'Grace is not just a doctrine to be believed; it is a fact you can lean your weight on.'*

Again we affirm that Acts is really about the Acts of the Holy Spirit, a truth further affirmed as we listen to their report. They talk about 'all that God had done through them', and 'God opening a door of faith to the Gentiles'. Sometimes leaders who have been mightily used of God, especially when the miraculous is involved, drift into an arrogant attitude, forgetting God alone is the source. We are simply conduits of blessing, and we can take encouragement, but not glory. That belongs to God alone.

Prayer: Living God, when I do well, help me to receive encouragement, but always remember my source. Amen.

Read:
Acts 14:26–27
Acts 11:22–24

FOCUS

'From Attalia they sailed back to Antioch, where they had been committed to the grace of God for the work they had now completed.'
(Acts 14:26)

*Wright, T., *Acts for Everyone, Part 2: Chapters 13-28* (London: Society for Promoting Christian Knowledge, 2008), p.35

Luke was there

One translation of the text describing this meeting includes the phrase 'when we gathered', suggesting Luke, the writer of Acts, was a member of the Antioch church, or at least present. Luke was a 'dear friend' to Paul. He is described as one of Paul's 'fellow workers' in verse 4 of Philemon, and recurs in 2 Timothy 4:11. He was probably a Gentile convert, and his education, research and careful writing gave us the book of Acts, and the Gospel bearing his name. It is thought that he probably joined Paul on a couple of his missionary journeys, but further details of his life are unknown.

The church in Antioch was blessed with riches of talent and gifting. Those who truly have a gift need to be recognised by the church before that gift is released into the church, otherwise there will be chaos, and just because we think we are gifted doesn't make us right. But are there gifted people in your church whose gifts are not being used? Are you one of them?

To ponder: Do you agree that those who truly have a gift need it to be recognised by the church before it is released?

Time to rest

FOCUS

'And they stayed there a long time with the disciples.'
(Acts 14:28)

Their first missionary journey behind them, it was time for Barnabas and Paul to rest and recuperate – remember Paul had almost lost his life when he suffered at the hands of the mob in Lystra. Perhaps there were wounds that needed to heal – Paul would write about the scars on his body ('From now on, let no one cause me trouble, for I bear on my body the marks of Jesus' (Gal. 6:17). There was the emotional cost of their tour, with the highs of miracles, responses, and the joys of planting churches, and the lows of pressure and rejection which must have taken their toll. As we read that they stayed in Antioch for 'a long term', Luke uses a word suggesting at least a year, although some commentators think it might have been four years. Rest and rhythm in our lives are so important; we need to take time for replenishment.

Tom Paterson, the creator of the LifePlan process, suggests we check we are refuelling our lives spiritually, emotionally, intellectually and physically. It can help us to check our 'tanks' in each of those areas, but should not lead us to compartmentalise our lives. A walk in the park can be physically useful, emotionally replenishing, help our spirituality and our relationship with God, and even help us intellectually if we learn something during our stroll! Some of us (including me) feel guilty when we relax. But if we don't obey Jesus' call to come apart and rest a while, then we will come apart.

Prayer: Lord of the Sabbath, help me to live in a healthy rhythm of work and rest. Amen.

take time for replenishment

A conflict with the apostle Peter

Read:
Galatians 2:11–13
Acts 11:1–18

FOCUS

'When Cephas came to Antioch, I opposed him to his face, because he stood condemned.'
(Gal. 2:11)

We turn now to an incident that happened in Antioch that Luke omits, but Paul describes as he writes to the Christians in Galatia. It was a visit from Peter to Antioch – a visit that went horribly wrong. Peter knew the way of Jesus was the way of full inclusion. During his amazing three-year journey with Jesus, Peter saw how He angered the Pharisees because of His insistence on having table fellowship with those considered untouchable. And then Peter had experienced the amazing vision where he had been told not to call anything unclean when God had called it clean. And so by the example and revelation of Jesus, Peter knew the Gentiles were welcome at God's table, and therefore they should be welcome at his. But previously he had got into some serious hot water over eating with Gentiles, and had to explain his actions when he returned to Jerusalem. Peace came, but only temporarily, and now in Antioch Peter bowed to pressure from a visiting, so-called 'circumcision group', and so withdrew from eating with Gentile believers. This rightly earned him a blasting from Paul. The Greek text suggests that Peter's withdrawal from his Gentile brothers and sisters was gradual, but withdraw he did. Peter's actions show us that yesterday's revelations and obedience do not guarantee we will carry on living according to that revelation or be obedient today. Let's remember what we have learned in the past, and ensure we are still being faithful.

Prayer: Lord, show me when Your principles are being eroded in my life, and enable me to live in the good of them each day. Amen.

Certain men

Read:
Galatians 2:11–12
Acts 11:22–24

All was going well in the church until a new family arrived. I was very young, and newly in ministry, and so was quite thrilled to welcome them. They were gifted, knew the Bible well, and seemed to be very, very spiritual. And that was the heart of the problem. It didn't take long before the criticism started. We were using the wrong version of the Bible, they said. Our worship was shallow, (How do you measure that?) we didn't pray enough, (Do we ever?) and they didn't experience the same sense of God's presence they'd had in the (many) churches they'd previously attended. It did not occur to me to ask why they had left those churches, and I later discovered a similar pattern in their history. Because of their air of superior spirituality, they drew others into their circle, which created other problems. I don't think that they intended malice, but theirs was a passionate spirituality turned toxic.

Something similar happened in Antioch, as we saw yesterday. Peter's decision to withdraw from the Gentile believers there – a decision that must have been devastating and confusing to those shunned – was driven by the influence of these unwelcome visitors. If trouble seems to follow you, whichever church you are in, perhaps it is time to ask why that is. It is possible that a change of heart and attitude is needed. I want the church I am part of to be strengthened because I am there, as happened when Barnabas came by.

Prayer: Lord, I want to bring blessing, not hurt; kindness, not carping; encouragement, not despair. May it be so, today. Amen.

FOCUS

'For before certain men came from James, he used to eat with the Gentiles.'
(Gal. 2:12)

Even Barnabas

Read:
Galatians 2:11–13
Acts 9:1–27

FOCUS

'The other Jews joined him in his hypocrisy, so that by their hypocrisy even Barnabas was led astray.' (Gal. 2:13)

Over the last few days Kay and I have been engaged in a stocktaking mission. Travelling in ministry, we keep hundreds of copies of books I have written, to make them available when we tour. A lot of effort was required to work our way laboriously through countless boxes to clarify exactly what supplies we have. Surely something similar should be ongoing in our lives. In reflection, prayer, conversation with others, and examining ourselves in the light of Scripture and with the help of the Holy Spirit, we should take stock of our strengths and weaknesses. Failure to do so may mean we blunder into some very poor decisions. As we read that 'even' Barnabas was led astray by this awful development in the Antioch church, not only do we see the power of influence (what we do can lead others into difficulties if they follow us along a path of folly), but also that our weaknesses can flow from our strengths. Barnabas was a warm soul, eager to bring harmony and conciliation. He had stood by Saul back in Jerusalem and vouched for him when the apostles were terrified of him. He would be the one to stand up for John Mark, whose failure during the first missionary journey led to Paul not wanting to give him a second chance (Acts 15:36–41). Perhaps too eager to pacify the Jerusalem church and hold everyone together, Barnabas withdrew from many of the people he had loved and pastored, a shocking sight. With God's help, let's take stock.

Prayer: Search me, and show me myself, Lord, both my weaknesses and strengths. Amen.

Confronting legalism

Legalism is teaching that leads us away from grace, into rules and regulations that are not biblically based but rooted in human tradition. Often those rules develop into fences, to help us avoid sin. Here is an example: there are some movies that Christians should not watch; their content is plainly at odds with the call to wholesome thinking the New Testament tells us to cultivate. But if someone (usually a leader) takes that truth and restates it to imply it is sinful to go to the cinema, then legalism has crept in. If that sounds extreme, remember previous generations of believers laboured under these prohibitions. Not only were some of the rules illogical (Don't go to the cinema, rent the film on video), but they took people away from the simple truth of being saved by grace. When people start to spread the virus of legalism in the church, it can be very difficult to confront, and doing so can sound like compromise. Paul reveals just how far he is prepared to go when it comes to defending the freedom explicit in the gospel – he would go head to head with even Peter himself, a huge step considering the time Peter spent with Jesus, and his place of leadership in the Jerusalem church. Peter and Barnabas' withdrawal from table fellowship with the Gentile converts in Antioch threatened to undermine the core truth of the gospel, and Paul would have none of it. Neither should we.

FOCUS

'When I saw that they were not acting in line with the truth of the gospel, I said to Cephas in front of them all...'(Gal. 2:14)

Prayer: Lord, I want to be holy, but never bound by legalism or guilty of propagating it. Show me Your ways. Amen.

Let's talk

'When they came to Jerusalem, they were welcomed by the church and the apostles and elders, to whom they reported everything God had done through them.' (Acts 15:4)

It is difficult to clarify the chronology of the unfortunate incident in Galatians 2 and this meeting, but the two events are obviously related. However it happened, though, Church history had reached a critical point. A conference was needed to settle the matter of relating to the Gentiles, and Paul and Barnabas travel 300 miles to Jerusalem, which may have taken a month. They were warmly welcomed.

This shows the Early Church was willing to engage in difficult conversations. We don't always do so well, rushing to label each other when anyone takes a position on doctrine that is different from our own. I want to be part of a church that can wrestle with 'hot potato' issues with grace and maturity. Travelling that distance proved the apostles were totally determined to find a way forward and explore the issues at hand at length. May we be a people who can 'go the extra mile' and debate and disagree with grace, and not shrink away from contentious issues.

To ponder: Why do we Christians often shy away from difficult conversations? How might we disagree agreeably?

Weekend

Learning and growing

Read:
Acts 15:5–11
Proverbs 27:6

FOCUS

'Now then, why do you try to test God by putting on the necks of Gentiles a yoke that neither we nor our ancestors have been able to bear?' (Acts 15:10)

We saw earlier that Peter's behaviour in Antioch showed he had either forgotten the lessons of his rooftop vision and his experience with Cornelius and his household, or he had chosen to ignore them. Perhaps it was simply fear that made him decide not to live in the good of what must have been a powerful event. But we can all change, learn and grow. Patterns don't have to be repeated throughout our lives. I have said it before, but let me affirm: when we follow Jesus, change is not just possible, but inevitable. As we hear Peter's impassioned speech, arguing strongly there is no distinction between Jew and Gentile now, and so insisting circumcision is unnecessary for Gentile converts, we hear how intensely God feels about freedom from unnecessary burdens. The thrust of Peter's argument is God has chosen to work among the Gentiles, an argument from his missional experience, and to place legalistic burdens upon these new Christians would 'test God' – strong words indeed.

These words come from a man who has really seen the error of his ways. Now, as Peter addresses the church, he has learned from his mistakes in Antioch. Paul's stinging rebuke and his accusation of hypocrisy – also strong words – have paid good dividends. Do we learn from our mistakes, or do we just keep repeating them? Are we open to others to help us grow, even if their words, though faithful, are wounding to our pride?

Prayer: When I fall, redeem my failures, Father. When others lovingly speak painful truth, help me to truly listen. Amen.

change is...
inevitable

Another change of mind

Read:
Acts 15:12–21
Philippians 2:1–11

FOCUS

'When they finished, James spoke up: "Brothers, listen to me."' (Acts 5:13)

I t is such a miracle, it is worth pondering for another day. I don't think that we can grasp the monumental shift of thinking that was called for in the Early Church. The inclusion of Gentiles, without burdening them with Jewish initiation rites, was nothing short of a revolution. James, famous for his epistle that rightly insists authentic faith leads to good works, was claimed as a champion by the circumcision party. It seems (from Paul's comments) that a delegation had travelled to oppose the unconditional welcoming of Gentiles into the church, claiming James had sent them. Whether their claim was true or false, James was known to be cautious about this 'open door' policy. But he now addresses the church and is willing to shift his thinking. Those who are humble enough to admit a change of mind surely carry the greatest weight, and are worth hearing.

In our early years of ministry, we had a deacon in our church who opposed our proposal to change the church's governmental structure. He agreed to search the entire New Testament to see if he was wrong. Then he stood up at the church's annual general meeting to personally propose the changes, humbly saying that he had weighed his own arguments against what the Bible said, and changed his mind. His study carried weight, and his ability to be open and change his mind gained him the respect of the entire congregation. Have we made our minds up, but need to open them again?

Prayer: Father, grant me confidence in what I believe, but humility to accept where I might be wrong. Amen.

Voices of Prayer

Christians struggle with prayer. It is so important, yet can be so hard to do. And often we feel that others do it so much better than we do, while we can feel that we are lobbing snowballs at the moon. Maybe we feel God isn't interested, isn't listening. But whatever problem we face in our prayer lives, someone in the Bible will have faced it first, and so, in these notes, Jeff Lucas looks at what the Bible can teach us about communicating with our Heavenly Father, who so wants to hear from us. He draws on Abraham's prayers, the prayers of Hannah, the mother of Samuel, those of the angry prophet, Jonah, and, of course, the prayers of Jesus Himself.

WRITTEN BY **JEFF LUCAS**
MAY/JUN 2021

Life Every Day

Church History

Applying the Bible to life

CWR

Also available as eBook/eSubscription

Disturbing teaching

Read:
Acts 15:22–35
Luke 11:37–54

FOCUS

'We have heard that some went out from us without our authorisation and disturbed you, troubling your minds by what they said.' (Acts 15:24)

The church in Jerusalem was not just discussing an item of theology, of academic interest and little more. Truth shapes life, and what we believe about God determines the way we live. The outcome of the Jerusalem debate was critical for the future health of the church in Antioch and worldwide in decades to come. The influence of those legalists had 'disturbed' and 'troubled' the Antiochene believers.

Disturbed and troubled – that was me as a new Christian. I obviously don't regret my choice to follow Jesus at the age of 17, but I cannot pretend my life was either filled with joy or characterised by peace. Before I became a follower of Christ, I was a fairly neurotic, obsessive person, plagued with insecurities. Then I became a fairly neurotic, obsessive and insecurity-plagued Christian. It was no one else's fault – the teaching I received in those early years was full of grace and low on legalistic religion. Nevertheless I was desperately worried through most of my late teenage years, anxious that I would displease God and He would reject me, unhealthily nervous that I might take the wrong turn, and worn out by a perfectionist attitude that made me rush to guilt and struggle with forgiveness. It was a bewildering time, and my mind was certainly troubled. And that was what was happening in Antioch with the newly converted Gentiles: legalistic teaching was robbing them of their peace. Let's ensure the faith we share liberates, and doesn't oppress.

Prayer: Show me, Father, where religion seeks to place heavy demands that do not come from You. Amen.

A prayer request

I have been writing for *Life Every Day* for fifteen years now. I am grateful that, as I travel around, I often meet readers who encourage me to keep going! I have been challenged recently about my failure to ask for prayer, both for this ministry, and my work as a teaching pastor in Timberline Church, as well as other projects in radio, writing and speaking. As I read about the encouraging letter sent from Jerusalem to Antioch, the happy response it created, and the encouraging and strengthening ministry of two visiting prophets, a prayer request forms in my mind. Encouragement brings strength – the two are married together in Scripture. We see from this episode that the ministry of the prophet is not limited to foretelling the future under the inspiration of the Holy Spirit (as in the case of Agabus and the famine), but also involves forth-telling – the bringing of truth that is vital, relevant and timely, and thus prophetic. I'd like to ask you to pray that the fruit of my sitting down to tap away at a keyboard, or standing on a platform to speak, will be that God's people know His genuine, deep encouragement, their lives will be strengthened and their hearts emboldened. As we draw close to ending our study together, my prayer for you today, dear reader, is that wherever you find yourself in this lifelong journey right now, your heart is lifted and further resolved to follow Christ, faithfully, joyfully, all the way home.

Prayer: **May I bring Your encouragement and strength today, loving God.**

**Read:
Acts 15:30–34
2 Thessalonians
2:13–17**

FOCUS

'Judas and Silas, who themselves were prophets, said much to encourage and strengthen the believers.'
(Acts 15:32)

A place called home

Read:
Acts 15:30–35
Acts 18:18–22

FOCUS

*'But Paul and
Barnabas remained
in Antioch, where
they and many
others taught and
preached the word
of the Lord.'*
(Acts 15:35)

I am convinced we all need a church home, a community of people where we can know and be known; where others will share our joys and sorrows, our triumphs and our pains. It seems Antioch was that place for Paul as his ministry developed. Sadly his team was depleted because of the conflict that erupted and the subsequent loss of his companion Barnabas, but as we leave the church, we get a picture of the two continuing to serve there after other itinerants had moved on. Later, Paul would return there after further exploits during his further mission travels. By that time, Antioch was no longer his base, but it seems it was a place of anchorage for him as he continued his ministry journey. Paul was a man of incredible resilience and courage, but even he needed a harbour for his soul.

As we conclude our visit to Antioch, return with me to the moment when two visiting prophets ended their time in the golden city. When they departed, we read they were 'sent off by the believers with the blessing of peace to return to those who had sent them' (Acts 15:33). I am reminded of the beautiful closing words of the liturgy, 'Go in peace, and serve the Lord.' Those two prophets, so used to bless and strengthen the church, were sent on their way with the blessing of shalom, of peace. And, whoever you are, and whatever your current circumstances, I ask this blessing for you too: Go in peace, and serve Him.

Prayer: Father, thank You for the church I call home. When we frustrate each other, grant us grace to stay together, and peace as we do so. Amen.

Order form

5 Easy Ways To Order

1. Visit our online store at **waverleyabbeyresources.org/store**
2. Send this form together with your payment to: **CWR, Waverley Abbey House, Waverley Lane, Farnham, Surrey GU9 8EP**
3. Phone in your credit card order: **01252 784700** (Mon–Fri, 9.30am – 4.30pm)
4. Visit a Christian bookshop
5. For Australia and New Zealand visit KI Entertainment **kigifts.com.au**

For a list of our National Distributors, who supply countries outside the UK, visit waverleyabbeyresources.org/distributors

Your Details (required for orders and donations)

Full Name:	CWR ID No. (if known):
Home Address:	
	Postcode:
Telephone No. (for queries):	Email:

Publications

TITLE	QTY	PRICE	TOTAL
		Total Publications	

UK P&P: up to £24.99 = **£2.99**; £25.00 and over = **FREE**		
Elsewhere P&P: up to £10 = **£4.95**; £10.01 – £50 = **£6.95**; £50.01 – £99.99 = **£10**; £100 and over = **£30**		
Total Publications and P&P (please allow 14 days for delivery)	**A**	

Subscriptions* (non direct debit)

	QTY	PRICE (including P&P)			TOTAL
		UK	Europe	Elsewhere	
Life Every Day (Jeff Lucas) (1yr, 6 issues)		£17.95	£22.50	Please contact nearest National Distributor or CWR direct	
Total Subscriptions (subscription prices already include postage and packing)				**B**	

*Only use this section for subscriptions paid for by credit/debit card or cheque. For Direct Debit subscriptions see overleaf.

All CWR adult Bible reading notes are also available in single issue **ebook** and **email subscription** format.
Visit **waverleyabbeyresources.org** for further information.

Please circle which issue you would like your subscription to commence from:

JAN/FEB MAR/APR MAY/JUN JUL/AUG SEP/OCT NOV/DEC

Continued overleaf >>

How would you like to hear from us? We would love to keep you up to date on all aspects of the CWR ministry, including; new publications, events & courses as well as how you can support us.

If you **DO** want to hear from us on email, please tick here [ ]

If you **DO NOT** want us to contact you by post, please tick here [ ]

You can update your preferences at any time by contacting our customer services team on 01252 784 700. You can view our privacy policy online at waverleyabbeyresources.org

Payment Details

☐ I enclose a cheque/PO made payable to CWR for the amount of: £ _____

☐ Please charge my credit/debit card.

Cardholder's Name (in BLOCK CAPITALS) _____

Card No. ☐☐☐☐ ☐☐☐☐ ☐☐☐☐ ☐☐☐☐ ☐☐☐☐

Expires End ☐☐ ☐☐   Security Code ☐☐☐

Gift to CWR   ☐ Please send me an acknowledgement of my gift   **C** ☐

Gift Aid (your home address required, see overleaf)

giftaid it I am a UK taxpayer and want CWR to reclaim the tax on all my donations for the four years prior to this year **and on** all donations I make from the date of this Gift Aid declaration until further notice.*

Taxpayer's Full Name (in BLOCK CAPITALS) _____

Signature _____ **Date** _____

*I am a UK taxpayer and understand that if I pay less Income Tax and/or Capital Gains Tax than the amount of Gift Aid claimed on all my donations in that tax year it is my responsibility to pay any difference.

GRAND TOTAL (Total of A, B & C) ☐

Subscriptions by Direct Debit (UK bank account holders only)

One-year subscriptions (6 issues a year) cost £17.95 and include UK delivery. Please tick relevant boxes and fill in the form below.

☐ *Life Every Day* (Jeff Lucas)

Issue to commence from

☐ Jan/Feb   ☐ Mar/Apr   ☐ May/Jun   ☐ Jul/Aug   ☐ Sep/Oct   ☐ Nov/Dec

CWR Instruction to your Bank or Building Society to pay by Direct Debit

Please fill in the form and send to: CWR, Waverley Abbey House, Waverley Lane, Farnham, Surrey GU9 8EP

DIRECT Debit

Name and full postal address of your Bank or Building Society

To: The Manager _____ Bank/Building Society

Address _____

_____

_____ Postcode _____

Name(s) of Account Holder(s)

☐

Branch Sort Code

☐☐ ☐☐ ☐☐

Bank/Building Society Account Number

☐☐☐☐☐☐☐☐

Originator's Identification Number

| 4 | 2 | 0 | 4 | 8 | 7 |

Reference

☐☐☐☐☐☐☐☐☐☐☐☐☐

Instruction to your Bank or Building Society

Please pay CWR Direct Debits from the account detailed in this Instruction subject to the safeguards assured by the Direct Debit Guarantee.
I understand that this Instruction may remain with CWR and, if so, details will be passed electronically to my Bank/Building Society.

Signature(s)

_____

Date _____

Banks and Building Societies may not accept Direct Debit Instructions for some types of account